Carving Traditional Style Kachina Dolls

Tom Moore

Text written with and photography by Molly Higgins

Schiffer Publishing Ltd

4880 Lower Valley Road, Atglen, PA 19310 USA

Dedication

This first book is dedicated to my children. Kim, the oldest, was always my shadow in the shop; Joe, a talented wood carver, his wife Tami also a carver; and the future generation of wood carvers, my grandchildren. Thomas, at age 11, has already earned his first ribbons for wood carving. Alex, has just started carving; and Tasia, Jimmy, and Jared have yet to take up the knife and gouge.

Acknowledgments

I am in great debt to those who have made this first book a reality. I would like to thank Cleve Taylor for his timely advice and encouragement; Mike and Shelly Colson, life long friends who have pushed and encouraged me in my art all these years; and Gerald Patterson, owner of Arrowhead R.V. Park, a true friend of wood carvers, whose enthusiasm for projects is an inspiration in its own right. I also want to thank Kathleen Schuck, owner of Wood n' Things, a friend, fellow carver, the person who really made this happen; and finally my wife Doris, who has and continues to endure all the wood chips I manage to transport from the studio into the house.

Designed by John P. Cheek
Type set in Seagull HV BT/Korinna BT

ISBN: 0-7643-1243-X
Printed in China

Contents

Disclaimer

It is important to me that I point out that I am not a Hopi nor have I been initiated into any of the Kiva societies. I do not consider myself an expert on the Hopi or Kachina ceremonies. However, I have the deepest respect for the Hopi and their beliefs. The material in this book is as accurate as I can make it at this time; any errors are unintentional, and not meant to inadvertently offend my Hopi friends.

Published by Schiffer Publishing Ltd.
4880 Lower Valley Road
Atglen, PA 19310
Phone: (610) 593-1777; Fax: (610) 593-2002
E-mail: Schifferbk@aol.com
Please visit our web site catalog at
www.schifferbooks.com or write for a free catalog.

We are always looking for authors to write books on new and related subjects. If you have an idea for a book, please contact us at the above address.

This book may be purchased from the publisher.
Please include $3.95 for shipping.

In Europe, Schiffer books are distributed by
Bushwood Books
6 Marksbury Ave.
Kew Gardens
Surrey TW9 4JF England
Phone: 44 (0)20-8392-8585; Fax: 44 (0)20-8392-9876
E-mail: Bushwd@aol.com
Free postage in the UK. Europe: Air mail at cost.
Please try your bookstore first.

Introduction

I have writen this book for beginning to intermediate wood carvers who would like to create an authentic kachina doll. The three kachina dolls in this book represent three different styles, and can be expanded upon by more advanced carvers. These dolls provide the carver with an opportunity to experience the creation of what is probably the oldest educational toy in North America.

I have spent many hours carving with First Nation carvers both here and in Canada. The stories we tell are included in this work in a small way. As you carve these dolls place yourself before the embers of a wood fire, soak in the humor and stories of other carvers, and enjoy the experience.

Kachina Dolls: What Are They?

Kachina carvings were originally intended to be dolls given to the young Hopi children. The dolls were meant to be played with and handled by children, and were equipped with cotton string so they could be hung from the log beams in the pueblo. The early kachina dolls were painted with earth pigments, and decorated with real feathers, shells, and fur. Dolls were posed in rigid positions with attention paid to the appearance of the the mask (so children could learn to recognize and understand them) and less attention paid to the costume and body. These dolls can be seen in the Heard Museum collection in Phoenix and other noted collections where kachina dolls are displayed.

After about 1940, trading posts and collectors began to put pressure on kachina carvers for more detailed carving, brighter paints, and more realistic dolls which would stand on their own or on bases. By the 1960s and 1970s the dolls had begun to assume dance poses, and to be extensively "dressed" with cloth or leather kilts, felt bandoliers and sashes, fur, shells, and lots of feathers. Navajos still carve "Hopi kachinas" in this style today.

By 1980, the Hopi carvers had begun to change over to all-wood kachina dolls, including even the carving of feathers and fur ruffs. This change was partly in response to the federal regulations regarding the use of feathers and fur. Many of the old kachina dolls had their feathers removed by nervous collectors. During this shift in style many of the best Hopi carvers started carving "kachina sculptures" which were never intended to serve as dolls in the old tradition. These carvings are not intended to be handled by children, but are exceptional works of art and highly accurate representations of the kachina. The attention to detail and the fact that they were being carved for a non-Hopi market caused some discomfort among traditional Hopi.

Recently a school of traditional kachina doll carvers has emerged centered around Sichomovi, a Hopi village on third mesa. The dolls they carve are in the 1940 tradition, with formal pose, earth pigment paints, and real feathers. Because of the pose of the arms of these traditional dolls, they are affectionately referred to as "belly-acher dolls". The carvings in this book will have the traditional belly-acher pose, however they also feature carved wooden feathers and the more recent brighter paint.

Tools Used

Flexcut Gouges	Harmen Palm Tools
FR 401 #5	1/4" 40° "V" Tool
FR 400 #3	1/8" 117m #4 "v" Tool
FR 306 #6	1/2" #3 Fish Tail Gouge
FR 600 #3	#9 Gouge

Detail Knife
Scalpel
Round Tip 1/4" Blade "Butter Knife"
Nibsburner with Tips KN-1, KN-3, or Spear Point
Dremel with 1/8" Round Burr and Sanding Sleeve

Paints Used

I prefer to use Delata Ceramcoat Acrylic Paints. With each of the projects I have listed the paint used along with its Delta number. Delta paints which could be used as substitutes are also listed by number after each name. In the event that Delta Ceramcoat paints are not available in your area or you prefer another brand, the numbers listed should allow you to use conversion charts available in craft and art stores.

Safety Note

When working on these or any other carving project, I strongly recommend the use of a carving glove. Gouges and V-tools can do a lot of damage with just one slip. I did not use a carving glove in most of the photos in this book in order to give a better view of what was being done at each step. At all other times, however, I do wear one, and so should you.

Corn Dancer

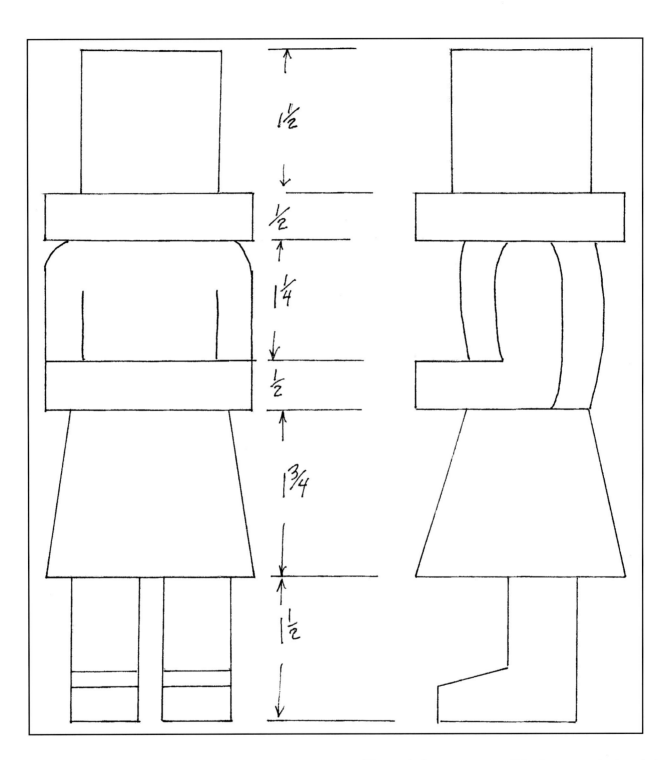

This is what I consider a classic kachina doll; you may choose to call it the stereotypical kachina. The Corn Dancers (there are serveral variations) all feature ear tabs, speaking tube, kilt, and sash.

The Corn Dancer is also known by the name Rugan, which is an adaptation of the Hopi word for rasp, a musical instrument that accompanies the procession of Corn Maidens and Corn Dancers. There are at least five variations of the Rugan or Corn Dancer.

The underlying purpose of Hopi ceremonies is to bring harmony to the world and successful harvests. The Corn Dancer represented in this carving is a Harvester Kachina and is associated with a good harvest of corn. The carving will feature a speaking tube, ear tabs, and the carving of a four-feather headpiece common to all corn dancers.

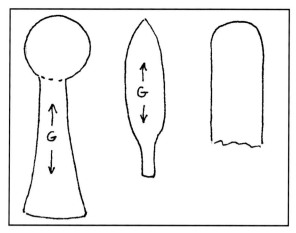

Accessory parts

Paints Used

Delta Number	Substitutes
2012	Turquoise
2506	Black
2059	Light Blue (2478/2069)
2503	Bright Red (2076/2083)
2027	Bright Yellow (2504)
2127	Dark Flesh (2033/2085)
2052	Kelly Green
Liquitex	Gesso (white)

Parts Used

Speaking Tube	1/2" dowel, 1/2"long
Ear tabs	1/8" thick, 1/2" x 1/2"
Four feathers	(see pattern)
Top knot	(see pattern)

Using a pencil, I have transferred the pattern (found on page 4) to a block of basswood measuring 2 1/4" x 2 1/4" x 7".

This is the top. Draw two lines from corner to corner to determine where the center of the block is. It's important to have the center marked like this to make sure the head is round and the figure is symmetrical.

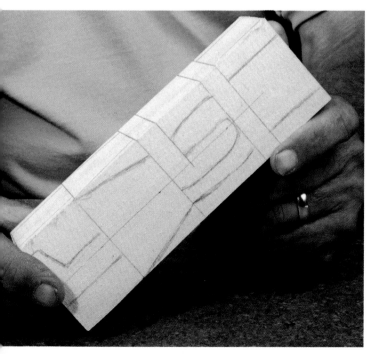

Now we can cut out the excess wood using the bandsaw, which has a 1/4" skiptooth blade. Make all the horizontal cuts first. This horizontal cut only goes as deep as the front of the leg.

The one from the back goes as deep as the back of the leg.

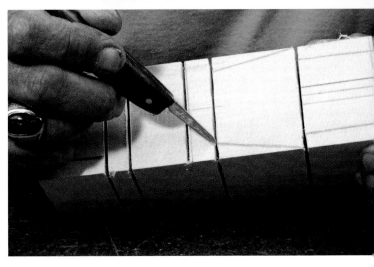

Cut only as deep as the skirt lines allow.

Cut only to the sides of the leg.

Horizontal cut to the chest.

Cut in to the front of the waist, under the arms to the kilt line.

Make a horizontal cut to the front of the mask.

Horizontal cut to the back of the mask.

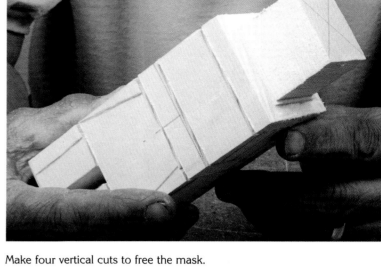

Make four vertical cuts to free the mask.

Horizontal cut to the back.

Once the horizontal cuts are made, we can make the vertical ones. Cut out the space between the legs.

Turn the doll over a quarter turn: this is the front of the figure. Make a cut in to the side of the mask, and repeat on all four sides.

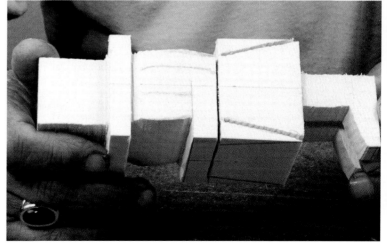

Here I freed the legs as well as the excess around the chest and back.

7

I've made the cut for the front and back of the kilt, but be careful not to cut all the way through or the figure won't sit level on the bandsaw table when you make the last two cuts for the sides of the kilt.

Now we're ready to get the knife out!

Once you've cut the sides of the kilt, the incomplete cuts will just break right off.

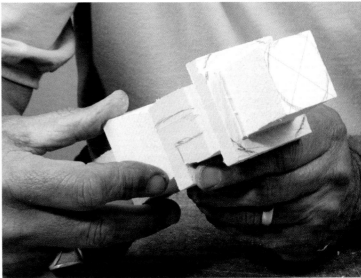

Before I cut, I'll make more markings for the arms, roundness of the mask, and the ruff. I like to mark reference points and guide lines frequently.

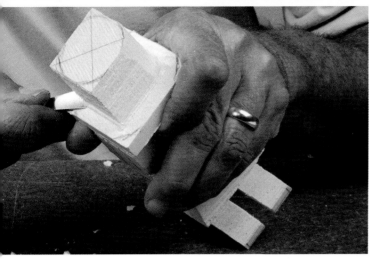

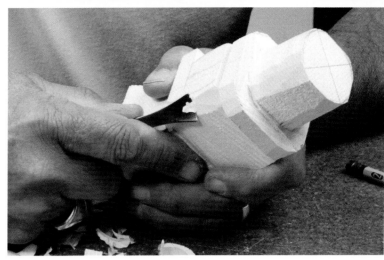

It's a good idea to knock the corners off first, so they don't bite into your hand as you hold the figure. Start at the top, with the mask, and work your way down. I'm using a fishtail gouge to make a plunge or stop cut at the base of the mask...

Now on to the back.

...and then I cut down to it.

I need to use the plunge or stop cut technique for the chest, first making a deep cut and then cutting down to it. These cuts also begin forming the arm.

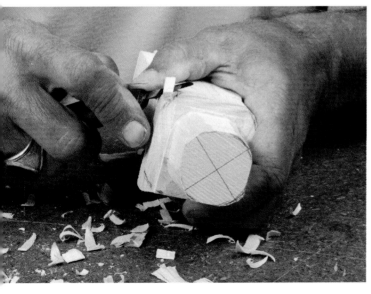

Now I'm rounding the corners of the ruff.

Round off the sharp corners of the kilt.

This Hiser #8 knife (butter knife), or any round tip knife, is great for taking off saw marks.

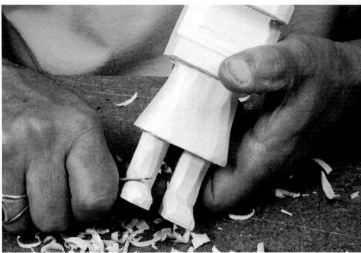

I'm rounding the corners on the legs with careful upward cuts with the grain. Make sure you listen to your knife. If you're going against the grain, the knife will really want to dive into the wood.

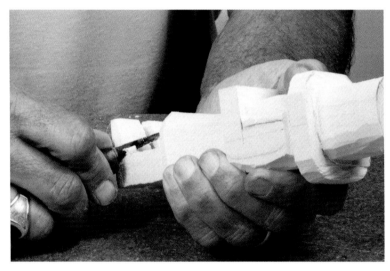

Be extra careful when you're working on the feet. This is the weakest part of the whole kachina. I take advantage of the strength of the wood by cutting from the toe to the ankle. Rest the figure on the table and cut up at an angle. Take care not to cut directly up or down...I have seen a lot of kachina dolls with broken feet!

Progress on the feet.

Round the toes off at an angle, too.

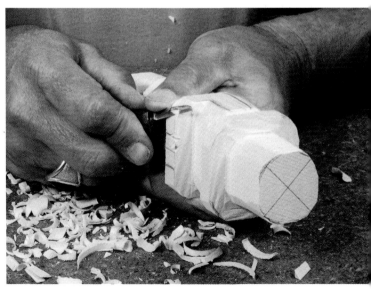

Let's move back up for some work on the hands. Start by rounding off the corners.

Using the fishtail gouge, I'm making a deep cut to mark the edge of the fist.

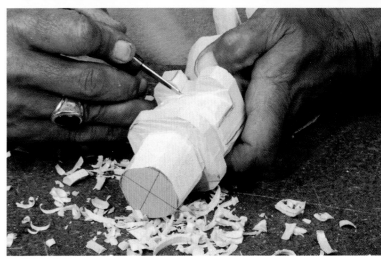

Use the knife to clean up the edge.

Then I make another cut starting at the center line between the hands, which knocks out a piece and pulls the hand away from the body.

I'll use a large V-tool to define the back of the arm.

When you get rid of the wood between the hands, make sure there's enough wood left in that space for the belt.

Progress.

11

Use the knife to clean up your cuts.

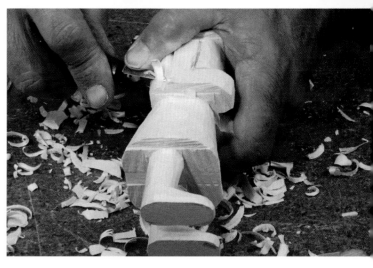

Cut the wood away with the knife, cutting along the edge of the straight cut.

Do the same for the front of the arm.

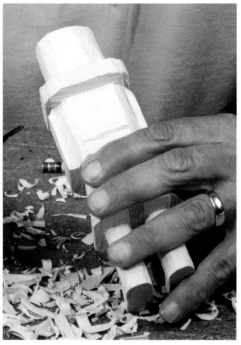

Progress: back view.

In the trench you made with the V-tool, make a straight cut.

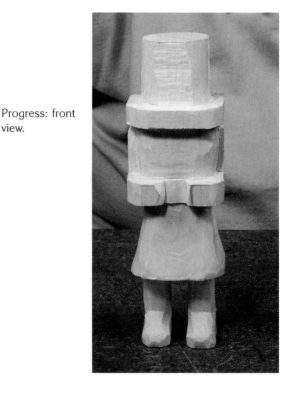

Progress: front view.

Using the same large V-tool, I am making a cut to define the belt on the back of the figure.

Smooth the arms.

Using a paring motion, cut down along the back towards the cut along the belt with a slight taper to give the belt a snug-fitting appearance. The round-tipped knife works well for this job.

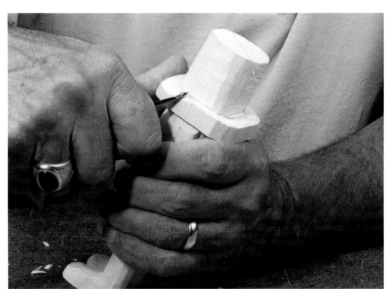

Smooth out the ruff by carving the corners off.

Round off the elbows.

Now I'm removing the saw marks on the mask.

Smooth the ruff into the base of the mask.

Continue to round the sharp edges until you're satisfied, and then we can begin the more detailed carving.

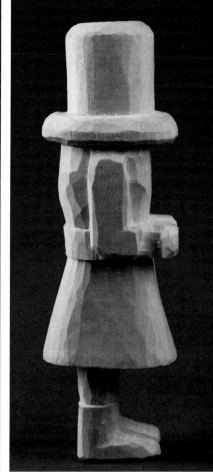

Progress

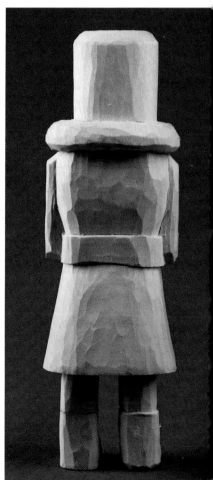

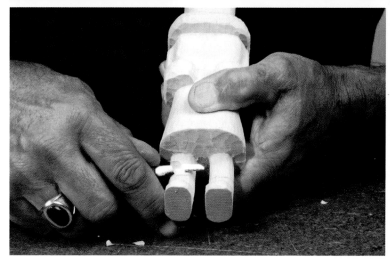

Start with the texture on the ruff. There are a lot of ways to do that. I use a small V-tool to make small cuts from the edge of the ruff in towards the mask. Make sure to vary the cuts so that it doesn't look like a ribbed turtleneck.

With the same knife, pull wood away above the moccasin to make the leg look more slender and fit into the moccasin.

Mark the top of the moccasins on the legs.

Make another stop cut at the top of the leg, where it meets the kilt.

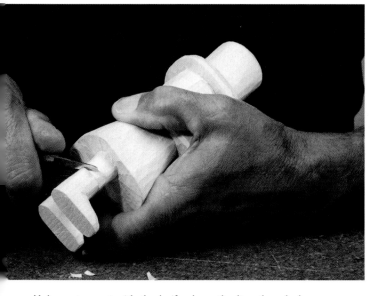

Make a stop cut with the knife along the line the whole way around the top of the moccasin.

Then cut up to it to shape the leg.

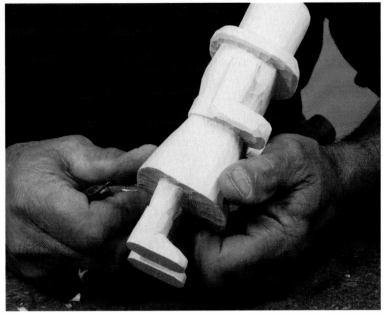

Progress.

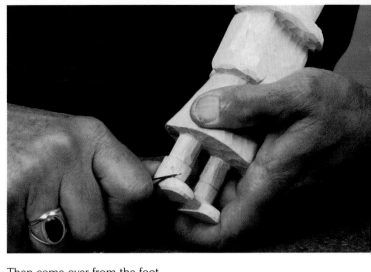

Then come over from the foot.

Round the bottom edge of the moccasin to shape it, but do it in small increments so as not to break the toe off.

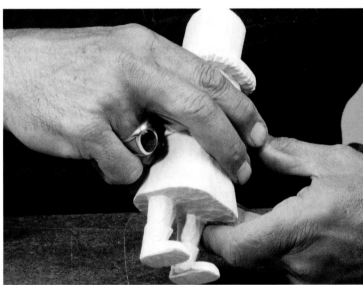

The finished feet.

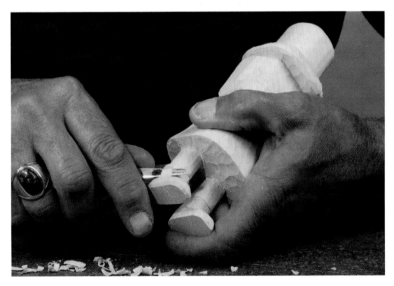

I like to notch the moccasin at the ankle, to make it look creased. I do this with two careful cuts. First come down from the direction of the leg.

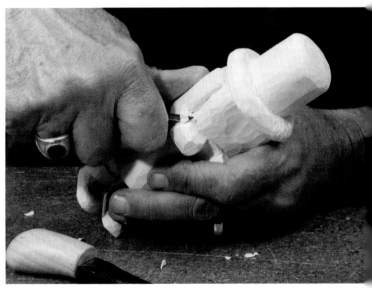

For the hands, I'm scooping out the area around the wrist with the detail knife.

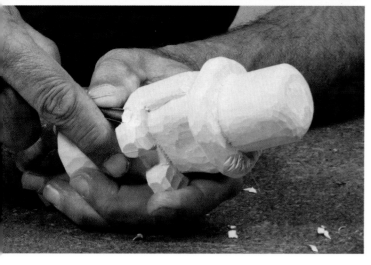

I'll use a Flexcut FR 306 #3 gouge to move around the side of it.

Using the knife, I'm rounding the hands and the arms.

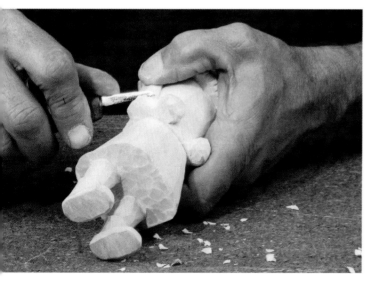

Make a crease where the forearm and elbow meet. Use two cuts to make a "v", one coming down from the upper arm, and the other from the forearm.

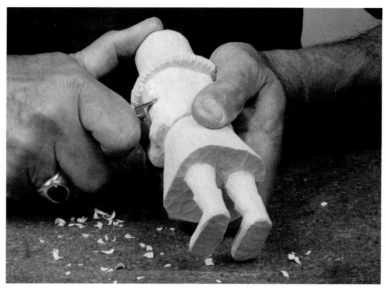

Rounding the upper arms.

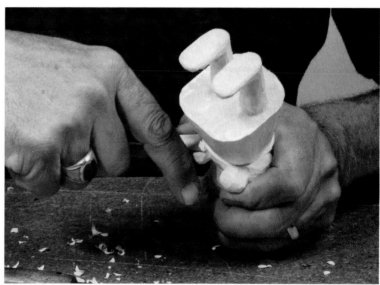

Use the fishtail gouge to clean up any knife scars on flat surfaces. Here I'm cleaning up the underside of the hand.

Now we're finished with the carving of the doll.

Now we can carve the smaller details. We'll do the feathers first. I like to use a wood that's stronger than basswood, since we're cutting it so thin—this is yellow cedar. You can also use walnut, yew, or some other hard wood. Using the bandsaw, make cuts that are 1/16" of an inch apart. If you do use basswood, make the pieces almost twice as thick.

Using the knife, pop the pieces off one at a time.

Draw the feather pattern onto the piece of wood.

Using the knife, carve out the outline of the feather...

...For something like this.

To make the feathers more realistic, we need to thin the edges. You can carve these by hand, but I've found it's much easier to use a Dremel tool with a sanding tip to bevel the edges. A Foredom, Ram, or other power carver willl work as well..

The thinned feather. Round the edges on the quill of the feather, using the knife.

For extra realism, I like to burn a couple of notches in the feather. Be careful not to overdo it!

I'm using a woodburner to mark the feather. First define the center line of the quill. Do that on both sides.

The finished feathers.

Starting from the quill mark and moving to the edge, burn in the vane of the feather. Do both sides.

Now I'm making the topknot. The key to this is to leave a handle. The round piece on the end is the topknot, and the center piece is what I can hold on to while I carve.

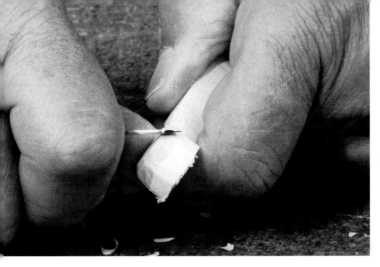

Using the detail knife, I'm rounding the topknot into a dome. Without the handle this would be much harder.

You might want to sand it a little. Now draw in the pattern of the feathers.

Progress on the dome.

Burn in the feather design. Burn as much as you can before cutting the handle off.

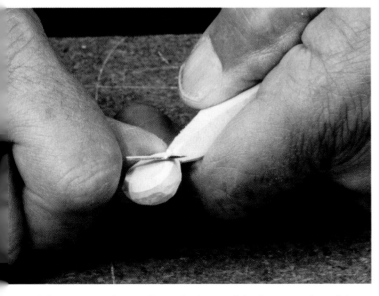

While the handle is still attached, round the bottom edge of the dome.

Using the knife, cut the handle loose. You could also use the bandsaw.

Finish burning the area where the handle was.

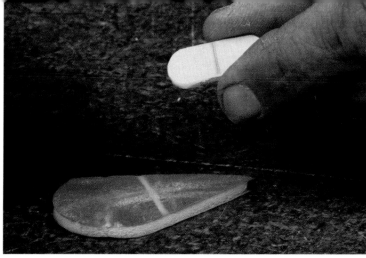

Sand the edges of the piece to make them smooth.

The burning is finished on the top knot and feathers.

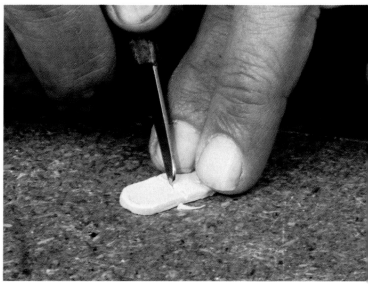

Cut the piece in half to make two ears, making straight cuts with a knife until the pieces are separated.

Now we'll do the ear tabs. We'll start with a piece of basswood the same size as a popsicle stick. Draw the tabs facing one another to make sure they're the same size. Round the edges of each tab, cutting the handle off.

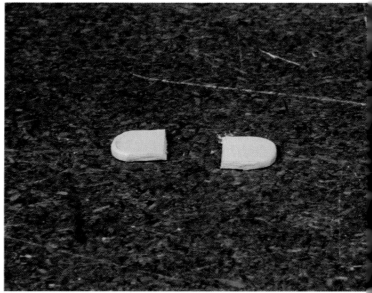

The ear tabs are ready to be attached.

For the speaking tube, I start with a 1/2-inch diameter dowel, on which I have marked off a 1/2-inch length. Using a Dremel with a 1/8-inch burr, I'm making an indentation to make the tube look hollow.

I like to mark the ears "left" and "right" to make sure each mortise I make is the right size. Start by making a small stop cut at each end of the mark, about the thickness of the ear tab.

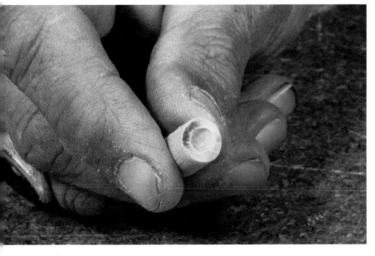

I used the bandsaw to cut off the tube at the line I drew, and sanded the rough edges. Then, using Titebond, glue the tube directly in place on the mask.

Make a cut between the two stop cuts, to form a letter "I".

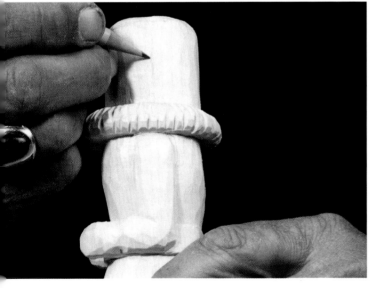

Let's glue in the ears. Using the arm as a reference, mark the mask where the ear will go. Mark both sides before you do any cutting, to make sure the ears will be even.

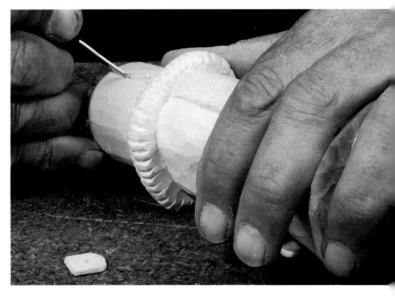

Right next to that cut, go in with the knife to take out a little piece of wood. Do that on both sides of the straight cut.

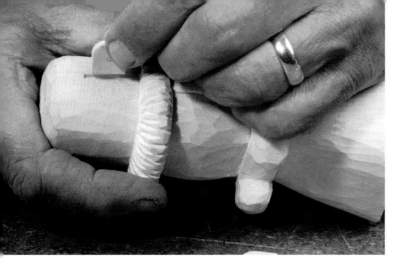

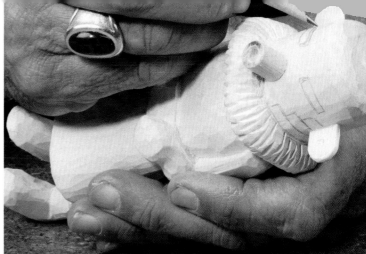

Check and see if the ear tab fits, and widen it some more if necessary. The tab should fit snugly.

Now I'm marking the designs for painting. I like to woodburn these designs in since it makes such a nice dark outline. There are full views of the designs on page 25. Remember that these are traditional markings, and that the colors and designs should be closely reproduced.

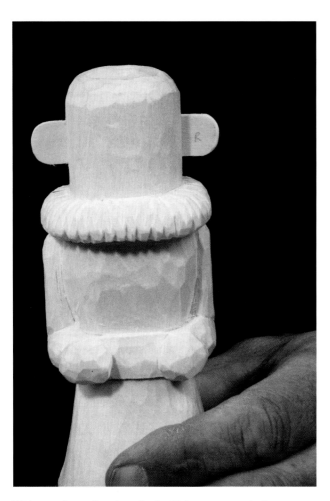

We're ready to glue the tabs in. Make sure you don't use too much glue.

Progress.

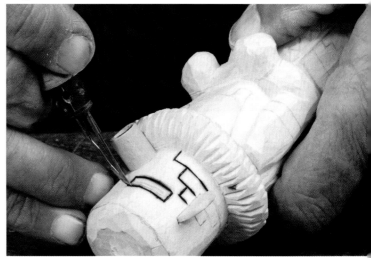

Now I'm starting the woodburning. Be very careful to make sure the eyes are an equal distance apart in relation to the tube.

I also am going to burn in the texture for the hair. Start by making a circle around the crown of the mask.

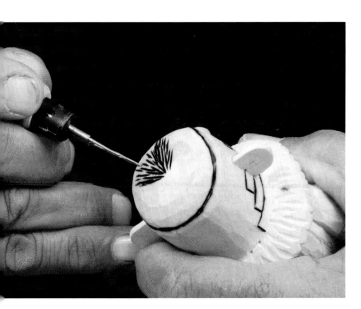

Start at the center of the mask and work outward, using short strokes.

Finishing the burning of the hair.

These are the designs that belong on the corn dancer.

Glue the top knot in place. It will need some time to dry before you can drill holes in it to put the feathers in.

Progress.

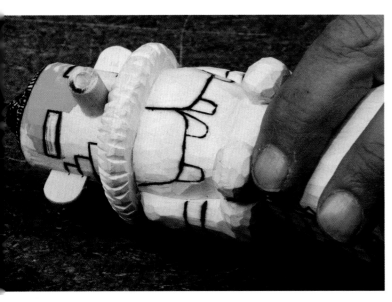

In the meantime, let's get started painting. I'm using Delta acrylic paints, diluted with water for a wash effect. I use the paint right out of the bottle—in fact, I use the lid instead of a palette. Brush it right to the edge of the burn line, but avoid brushing over. If you make a mistake, you can go in with the knife point or a toothpick to gently scratch the excess paint out of the burn line.

Once the glue is dry on the top knot, we will drill holes in it for the feathers. First drill one at the base of the knot.

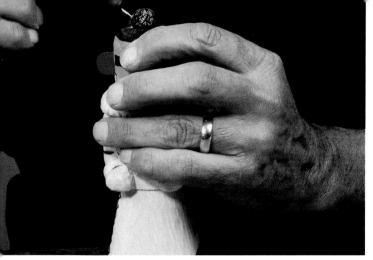

Then drill one on the topknot at this angle.

Progress.

Insert two of the feathers to help you visualize where to drill the two holes on the other side.

To paint the feathers, I use gesso. Paint it on thin enough that you can see the woodburned lines through it.

Now we can glue the feathers in.

Use black for the feather tips.

The finished doll. These are the colors to use for the corn dancer.

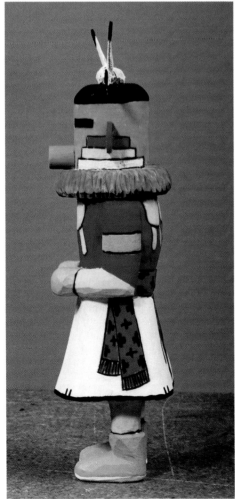

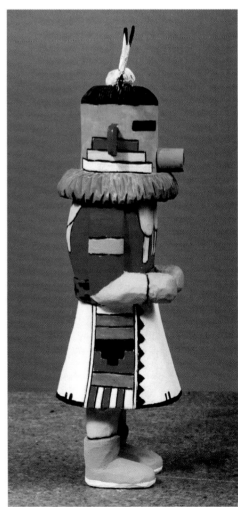

Polí Sío Hemís

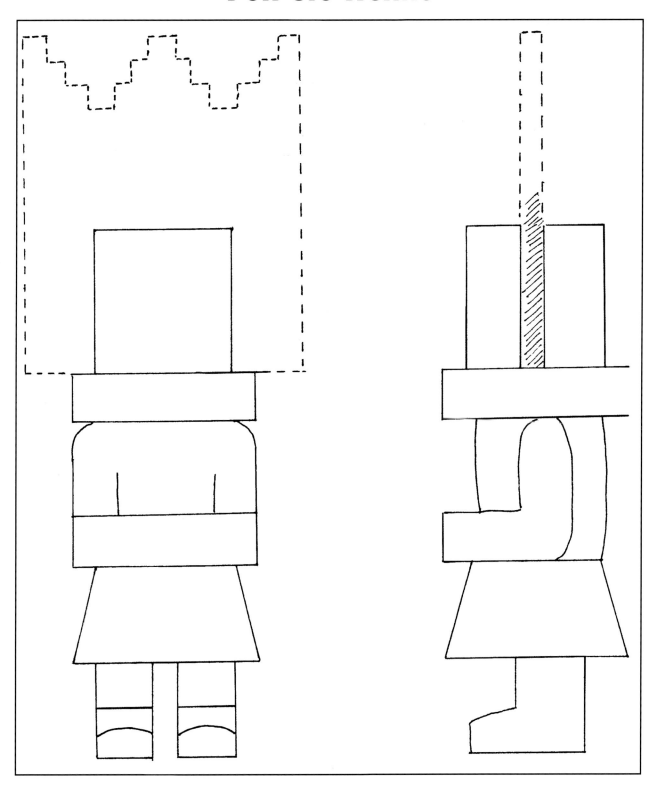

Some kachinas are traded back and forth between neighboring pueblos and the Hopi mesa top villages. The Zuni being the closest neighbors have many kachinas which move over into the Hopi ceremonies. Many of these trades or adoptions are the result of belief that the kachina has brought rain or other benefits.

Poli Sio Hemis represents the butterfly, which pollinates corn and the desert wild flowers. This is a Zuni kachina and closely related to the Third Mesa Poli Kachina. The Poli Sio usually appears in the ordinary plaza dance.

The carving of this doll will teach you how to carve a spruce bough ruff in more detail. The less adventuresome carvers can represent this ruff in the same manner as the Corn Dancer, or Rugan, shown earlier. The white sash in this carving is different from most kachinas, which have the more traditional red sash. In carving this kachina we will not only carve the sash but also the red bandolier. It is acceptable for carvers to also represent these by wood burning and painting.

Accessory parts

Paints Used

Delta Number	Substitutes
2051	Cobalt Blue (2038/2551)
2503	Bright Red (2076/2083)
2027	Bright Yellow (2504)
2050	Light Brown (2086)
2059	Light Blue (2468/2069)
2506	Black
2052	Kelly Green
2030	Burnt Sienna
2057	Pale Grey
2102	Butter Yellow (2504)
Liquitex	Gesso (white)
003 Micron	Archival Ink Pen (black)

Parts Used

Speaking Tube	3/8" dowel, 3/4" long
Tablet	1/4" x 3" x 3 1/2", Midwest brand

30

Lay out the pattern on a 2" square x 5 1/2" long block.

Lay out the tablet (using the pattern on page 30) on a piece of 1/4" x 3" piece of milled basswood. I like Midwest brand. Make sure the grain is running this way, as shown.

I have cut out the block and tablet using the bandsaw. For more advice on how to do that, take a look at how I cut out the Corn Dancer, page 7. Then round the corners and edges. (see page 9).

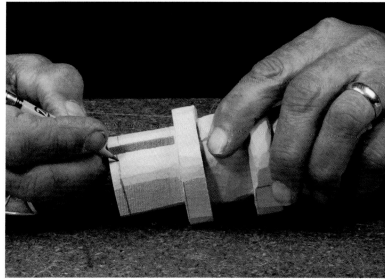

The top of the mask comes out slightly, so mark it all the way around.

To fit the tablet over the mask, we are going to cut a slot in the doll. Measure the width of the tablet and mark it on the blank. Try to place the tablet so it will pass through the center of the mask.

Run a V-tool all the way around on the line you just drew.

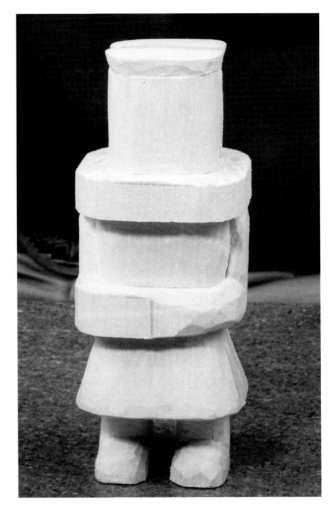

Progress.

Using the knife, cut from the top of the mask down towards the V-cut you just made, so that the top tapers into it to like a spool of thread.

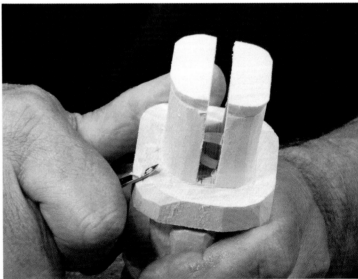

We're going to do the ruff a little differently, so I am only rounding the edges on the top side. Use a knife, a gouge, or a Flexcut FR 401 #5.

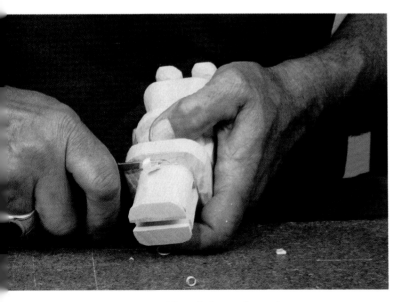

Cut away some wood from below to bring the top out more.

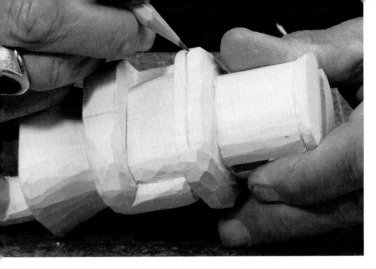

Once the top edge is rounded, mark a center line around the ruff—we are going to carve out another shelf in it.

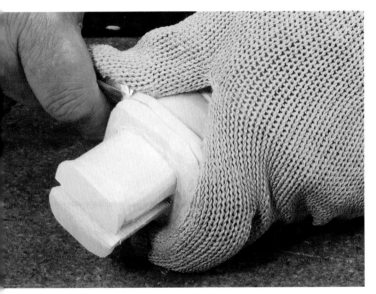

Use a V-tool to cut along the line.

With the "butter" knife, or round-tip knife with a 1/4-inch blade, cut up to the V-cut to widen the gap a little more. This can also be done with the detail knife; it's just a little more difficult.

Progress.

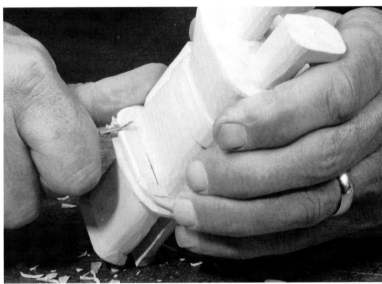

Take a little bit off the bottom of the ruff, just enough to round it so it's not sharp.

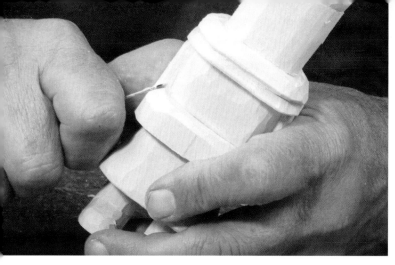

The hands on this kachina are also slightly different from the corn dancer—more in the traditional belly-acher style, with hands together close to the stomach. I'm rounding the edges on the arms some more.

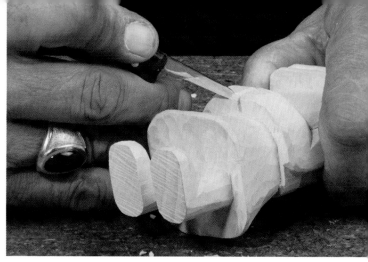

Knock off the corners where the knuckles will be.

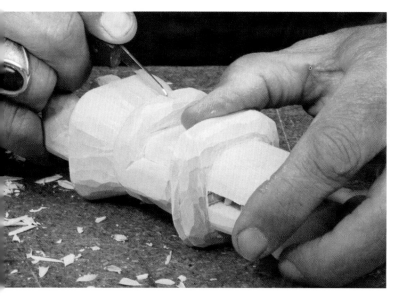

Make a straight cut where the hands meet.

Round the hands.

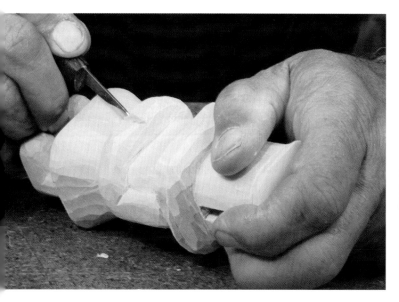

Cut away more wood by cutting from either side in towards the straight cut.

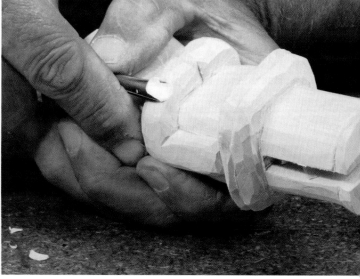

Use the gouge to scoop out some wood to create the wrist.

Progress.

Below: Draw in the bandoleer, the belt, and the armband.

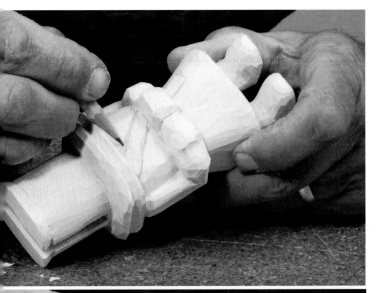

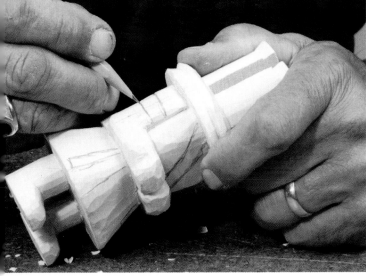

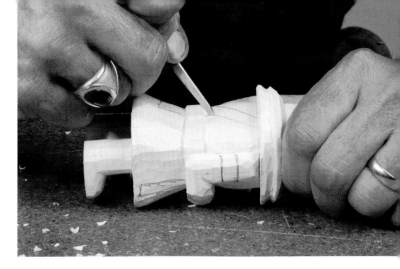

Since we're carving the bandoleer, armband, and belt, start by making a straight cut along the outer edge of the pencil lines.

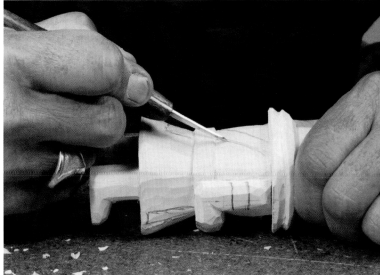

Make an angle cut in towards the straight cut outline.

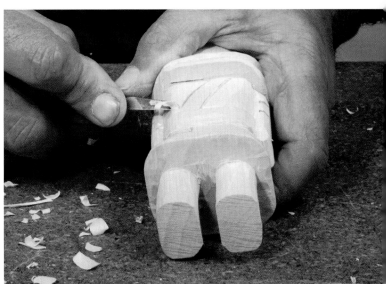

Then carve away wood around the bandoleer, belt, and armband to make them stand out.

35

The ruff on this doll is made from pine boughs, so draw them in.

Using the knife, notch the v-cuts out a little more from both sides.

Using a small V-tool, cut along the lines you drew from the edge of the ruff in towards the mask.

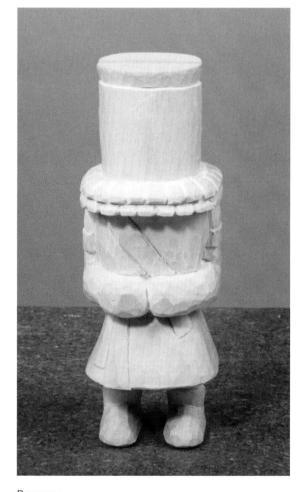

Progress.

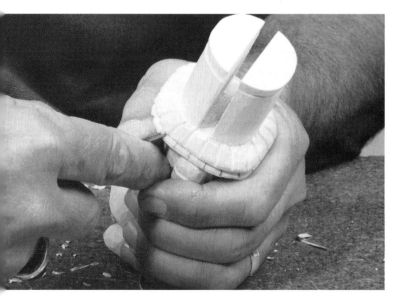

Draw more lines on the bottom part of the ruff and cut them out the same way.

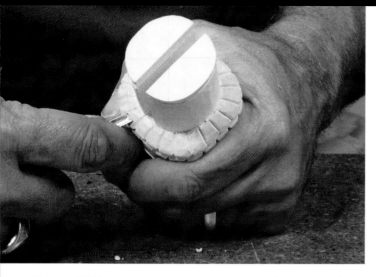

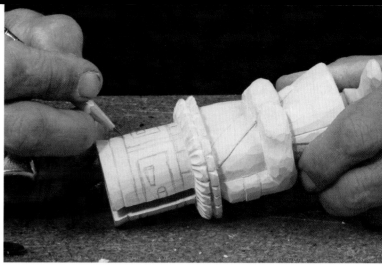

Using a #9 Harmen gouge, scoop out the area between each cut in the ruff so they become concave.

Now we can do some woodburning. First, draw on the design. (For pattern, see page 38)

Progress.

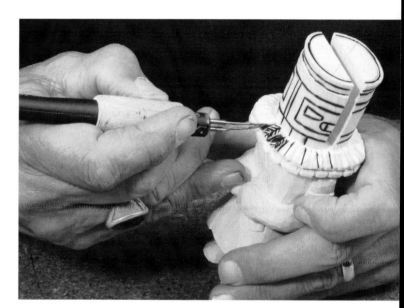

To texture the ruff, use the woodburner to first draw the pine boughs, then the needles.

Make a speaking tube with 3/8" diameter dowel, cut 3/4" long (for more detailed instructions, see page 23).

Progress.

Once the woodburning on the mask and ruff is finished, we can glue on the speaking tube. I'm using the end of a paper match to get rid of the excess glue.

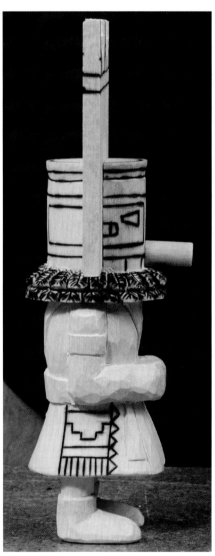

Now the woodburning is finished. Here are the designs that belong on the Poli Sio Hemis. Note that the tablet is *not* glued on yet.

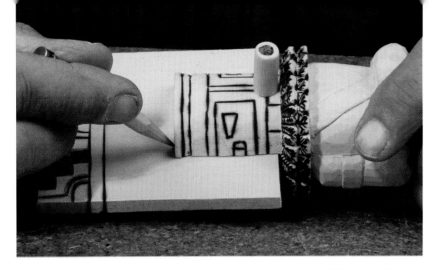

Draw lightly on the tablet around the outline of the mask, and label the tablet "F" for front.

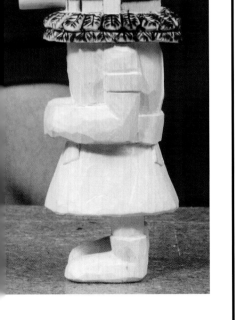

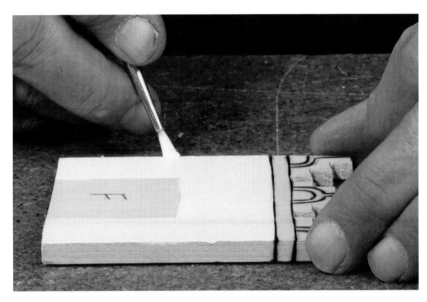

Now I'm covering the tablet with a layer of gesso. Try to coat it as smoothly as possible, since this is the main color for the tablet. I use gesso because it most closely replicates the white earth pigment paint used on early kachina dolls, and it covers anything.

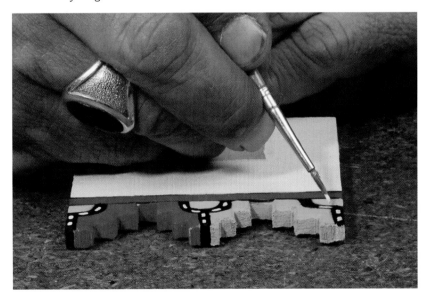

Fill in the top area with red, yellow, blue, and black to look like this. Use gesso to make the white dots over the black.

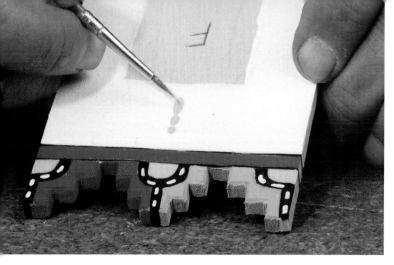

For the butterfly and corn images on the tablet, I start by putting the color down first and then adding the outline. Start with the butterfly body in gray.

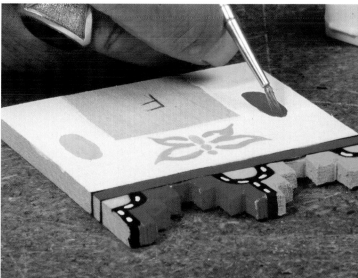

On the other side, paint a similar oval in red.

Then add the wings in blue.

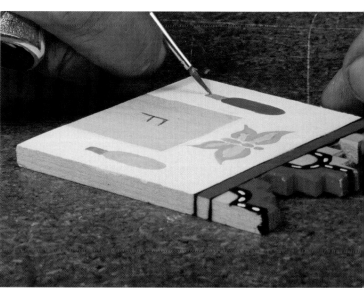

Add green for the stalks of the corn.

For the corn, paint an oval in yellow.

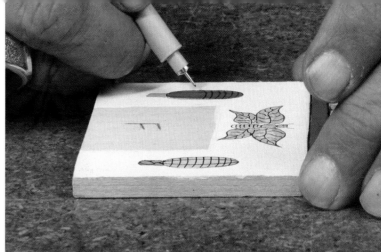

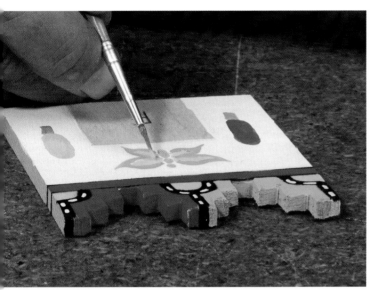

When the blue paint is dry, paint the inside of the butterfly wings yellow.

The corn also looks great with the outlines. Make sure you add a dot to the center of each kernel.

Then put the details on the butterfly. I like to use a Pigma Micron 005 #1 archival ink pen.

Now you can glue the tablet in place on the doll.

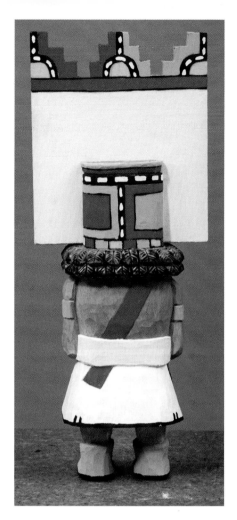

Here are the color schemes to use for the Poli Sio Hemis. Use a burnt sienna wash on the arms and chest.

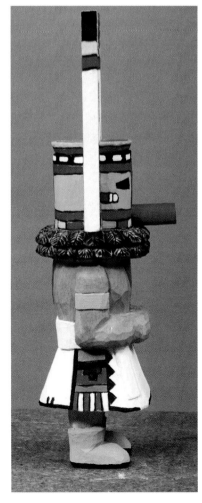

Crow Mother

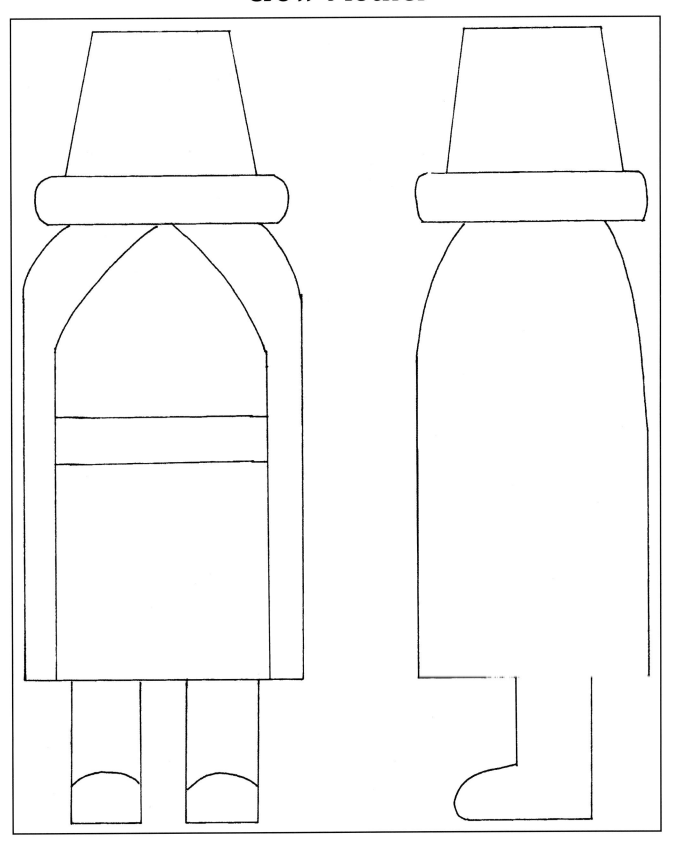

Paints Used

Delta Number	Substitutes
2052	Kelly Green
2506	Black
2059	Light Blue (2478/2069)
2503	Bright Red (2076/2083)
2027	Bright Yellow (2504)
2127	Dark Flesh (2033/2085)
2097	Brown/Dark Orange (2054)
2425	Beige/Dark Tan (2435)
Liquitex	Gesso (white)

Parts Used

Two Crow Wings	(see pattern)
Two Hands	(see pattern)
Four Yucca Whips	(see pattern)

Accessory parts

The third project in this book differs greatly in appearance from the first two. There are two varieties of this kachina, and the name "Crow Mother" will be used in discussing both of them unless the information pertains only to the Crow Bride.

The Crow Mother appears during the Powamu, or Bean Dance ceremony in February. The costume consists of a dress and woman's ceremonial robe. The dress of the Crow Mother is black, trimmed in green embroidery, and she carries yucca whips in her arms. The Crow Bride has a white dress and carries a bowl of corn. Crow Mother has blue women's moccasins while the Crow Bride wears white ones.

Crow Mother is the mother of all Whipper Kachinas (Hu') and some Hopi believe she is the mother of all kachinas. It is unclear whether the Crow Mother and Crow Bride are two separate kachinas or one kachina in two ceremonial roles.

Kachina dolls representing the Crow Mother were fairly common in the 1940s, but recently it is seldom carved and not often seen in galleries.

In carving the Crow Mother, you will have the opportunity to carve a robed kachina, add wings to the mask, and carve hands and forearms to hold either yucca whips or a bowl of corn. The ruff in this carving is fox fur. I have seen it carved with a spruce ruff, but the fox fur is preferred and may be the more accurate representation.

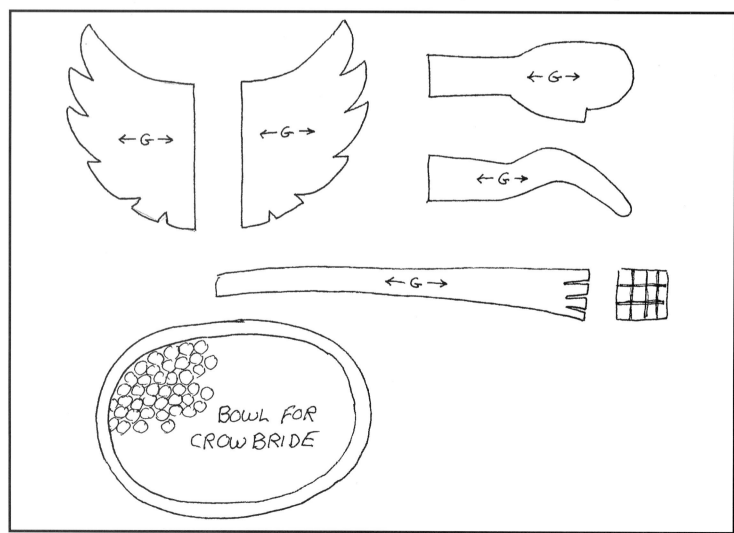

BOWL FOR CROW BRIDE

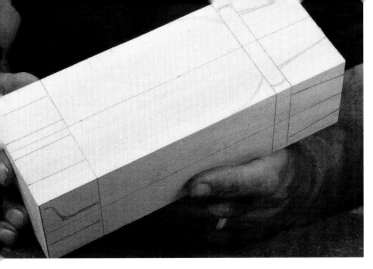

Begin with a block of wood measuring 3" x 2 1/2" x 8 1/4".

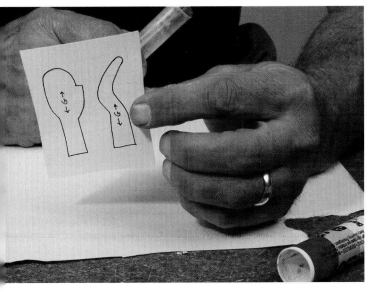

On this kachina, we're going to need to make templates for the hands and wings, as well as the yucca whips or the bowl. Photocopy the patterns on page 44 and cut them out.

Use a glue stick to glue the pattern to a file folder or other card stock.

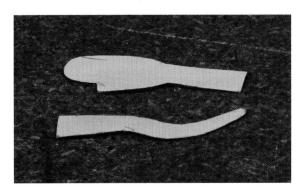

Use a small knife or sharp pair of scissors, and cut the templates out.

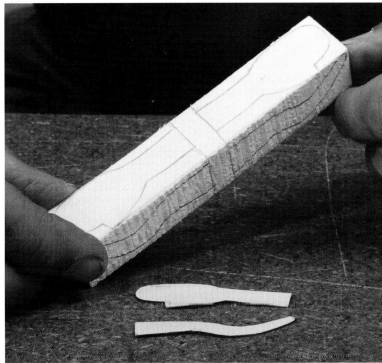

On a piece of wood 7/8" square x 5", draw the pattern for the hands. Note that there is a difference between the left and right...be careful not to carve two of the same hand!

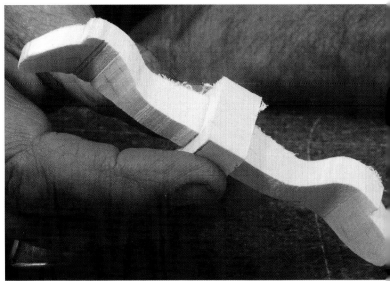

Bandsaw the excess wood out, but make sure you leave a handle in between.

45

Using 3/8" stock basswood, trace wing templates. Pay attention to grain direction!

Cut the wings out using the bandsaw.

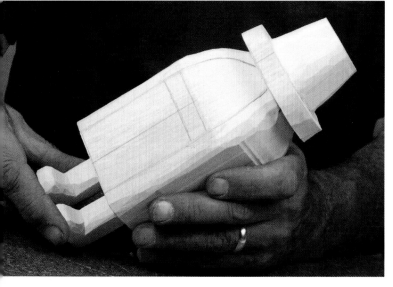

On the figure, cut out the excess with a bandsaw and then round off the corners (for a more detailed explanation, see page 9)

Take the corners off the ruff. I'm using a Flexcut fishtail-type gouge (FR 400 #3).

Begin the cloak by making a V-cut where the robe and dress overlap.

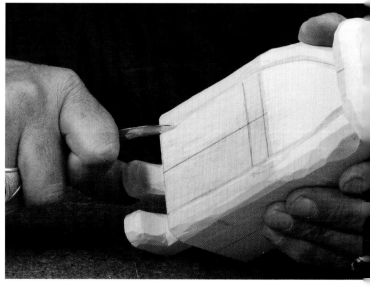

Make a straight cut along the depth of the V-cut.

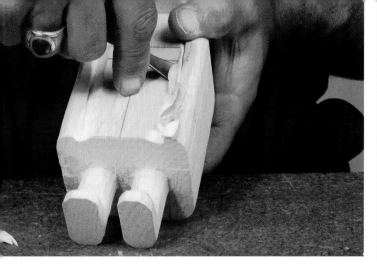

Using a fish tail gouge, scoop out wood in a motion towards the straight cut.

Make V-cuts along the marks to define the belt.

Make a stop cut at the neck under the ruff...

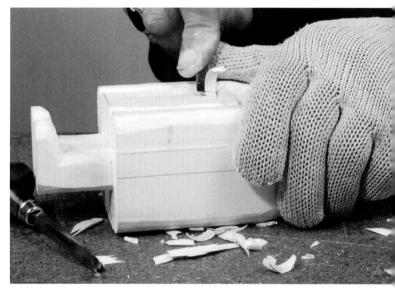

Remove wood above and below the belt line so that the robe stands out from the body.

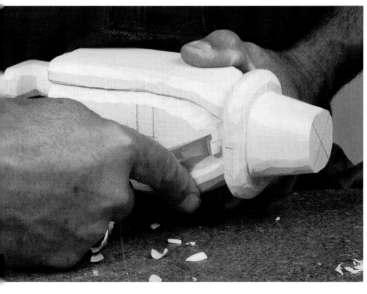

Then scoop out some wood from the chest.

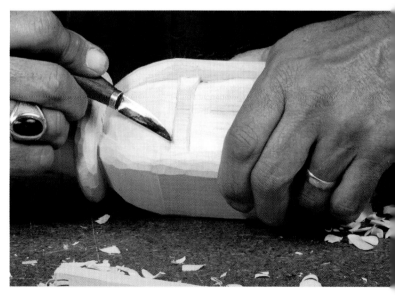

Progress.

Continue taking wood from the inside so the robe overlaps the dress more realistically.

The goal is to make the belt look as though it wraps around under the robe.

On the outer part of the robe, scoop away wood to give the appearance of the fabric draping over the arms, which will come out of the robe at the belt level.

Progress.

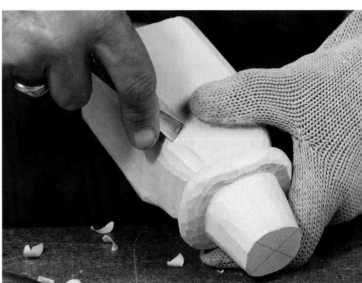

Rounding the shoulders.

Progress.

Then take off wood from the wrist, cutting toward the handle...

...and cut off the chips at the handle with one stop cut.

Let's move on to the hands. Take the back edge off first.

For the palm of the hand, start at the heel and stop at the palm.

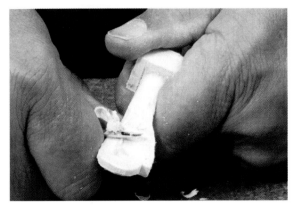

Remember that the grain changes direction, so turn around and start at the fingers to work back in toward the palm.

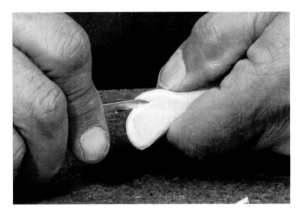

For the thumb, mark the place, and cut down over toward the palm. Again, the grain will not favor this, so be careful!

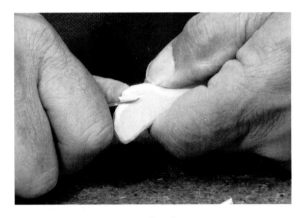

Then cut down to remove the chips.

Now all we need is a little sanding, and the hands are finished.

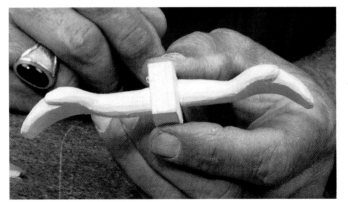

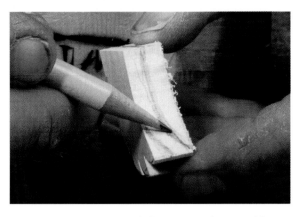

The wings should have a little curve to them, as I have drawn here.

The other wing should curve the other way, to make a right and a left. Draw them both at the same time and compare them, as it is easy to draw two of the same.

I made a z-board that's much better and safer resistance than my hand when I'm using the gouge for things like this. I am scooping wood out of the wing to give it the curved look.

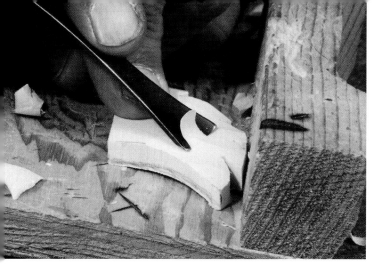

Remove the wood all the way to the line you drew.

Use the knife to round the edges and thin the wing a little more if necessary.

Flip the wing and add the curve to the other side.

Now we will define the feathers. I'm going to use the Nibsburner, and take a simple approach. You may choose to burn much more detail into the wing feathers.

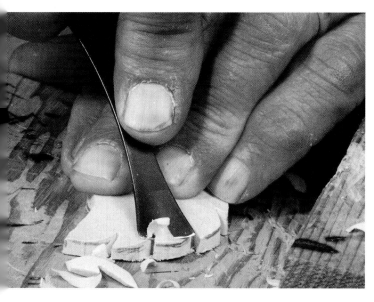

I like to bevel the wings so they're thin at the edge.

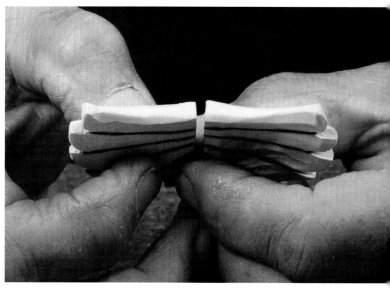

The wings are done for now.

I have separated the hands from the handle using the bandsaw.

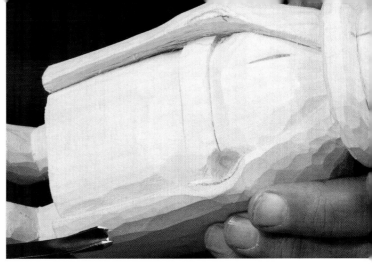

Progress. Make sure you check the fit of the hand where you've carved to make sure you don't carve too much away.

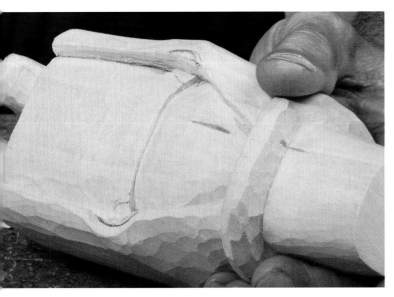

Now we are going to insert the hands on the doll. Mark the area where they will go.

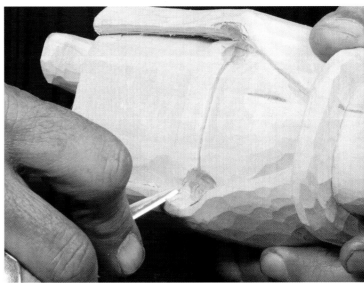

Thin the robe a little to make it look less heavy.

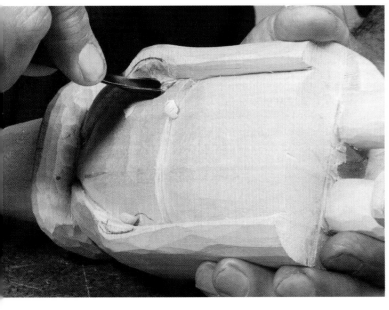

Carve away from the inside to create a slot for the wrists.

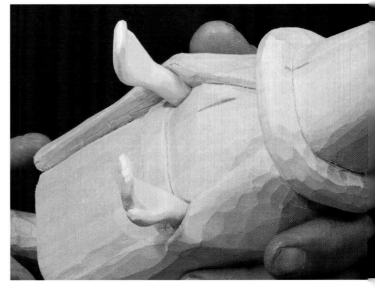

These hands stick out a little too far; I'm going to shorten them a bit.

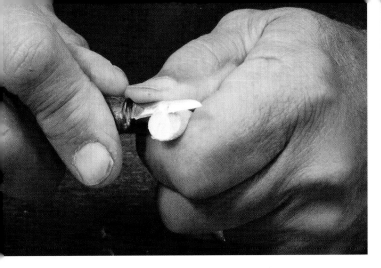

I'll use the knife to trim the arms.

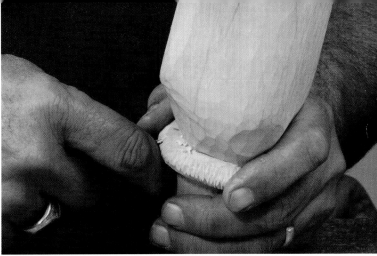

Make sure you get the underside of the ruff too.

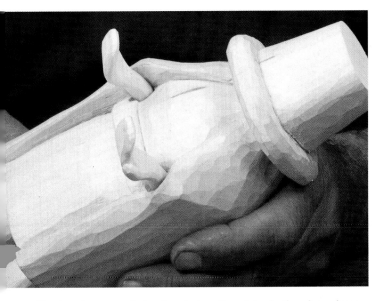

The hands are ready to glue, but we'll wait to do the gluing later.

Progress.

Now I'm adding texture to the ruff, to make it look like fur. I'm using a small V-tool.

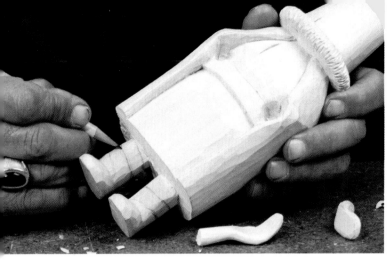

The moccasins need finishing. These are women's moccasins, so they're different from the ones on the other two projects. They wrap around the leg more. Start by marking a spiral around each leg.

To make it look like the buckskin is wrapped around over itself, take some wood away from underneath each spiral cut.

It's important to make sure the spirals start from the inside of the leg and move out in opposite directions.

Progress on the legs.

Make a straight cut with the knife along the lines you just drew.

Round the edges on the feet.

The finished feet.

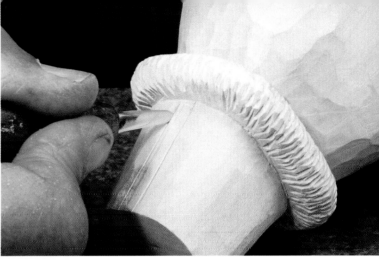

Make a straight cut along the outline of the wings you made on the mask.

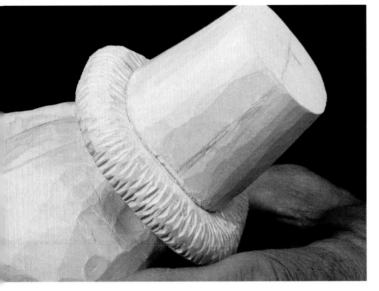

Now the wings need to be attached to the sides of the mask. It's important that the wings are centered on the sides of the mask and directly opposite one another. I'll mark the mask first.

Cut wood from the inside towards the two straight cuts, but make sure the outer lines stay straight.

The wing is the same size as the mask, so it will be much easier to mortise them on to the doll. Mark the thickness of the wings along the line where you first marked the mask.

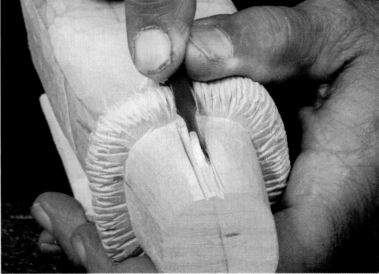

Now remove wood between the two notches. I'm using a Flexcut FR 600 #3 gouge. Make a stop cut first down at the ruff to make sure you don't take any wood out of the ruff.

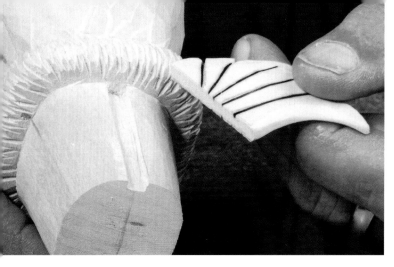

Check frequently to make sure the wing fits snugly in the slot; make sure you don't carve away too much.

This wing is ready, but we won't glue it in place yet.

These are some of the most common designs found on kachinas. This is the women's robe pattern.

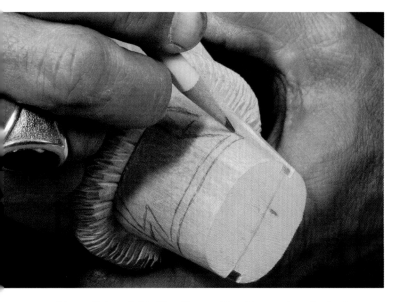
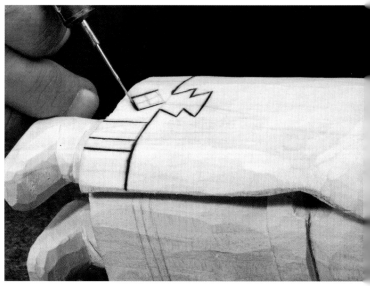

Above & top right: Now I'm marking the mask and robe for woodburning.

Woodburning the designs.

Left: Once the woodburning is done, we can glue the wings and hands in place. Here is a full view of the woodburned designs for the Crow Mother.

Now for the yucca whips. Cut at least five from the pattern. I'm rounding the blanks I cut.

Using the scalpel, cut away wood on the ends until they come to points.

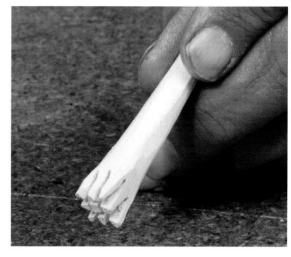

Progress.

57

I'm using the V-tool to make cuts along the length of the whips, to add the reed-like texture.

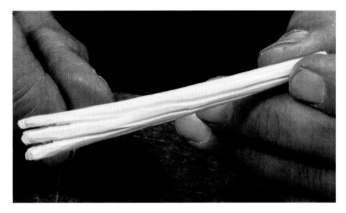

The finished whip.

Now we're ready to paint!

For the whips, I use a wash of kelly green.

While it's still wet, I work in a little white on both ends.

The painted yucca whip.

The ruff should be painted to look like fox fur. I start by underpainting it with gray. Use a lot of water to make a wash that gets into all of the little grooves you've cut.

For the over coat, use a shade of brown with red in it. Use a dry brush so that the gray still shows through.

The painted ruff.

The painted Crow Mother.

Glossary

Belly-Acher Doll The name Belly-Acher refers to the position of the arms tucked in close to the belly of traditional kachina dolls carved in the 1940s.

Case Mask & Sack Mask Kachina masks are mainly divided into case or sack masks. The *case mask* is a cylinder shape, much like a five-gallon ice cream container that sets down over the dancer's head. A *sack mask* is a hood or sack that is slipped over the head and tied at the neck.

Ear Tab Ears on many kachina dolls resemble the rounded end of a popsicle stick. This type of ear is referred to as an ear tab; the most common color is red.

Kachina Kachinas are the guardian spirits of the Hopi. These spirits have power to affect nature, weather and rain which is very important to the desert dwelling Hopi.

Kachina Kilt The skirt or kilt which is worn by the kachina and whose designs have ceremonial significance.

Kiva The kiva is a circular underground room used for ceremonial purposes. The Kiva is entered by a ladder in the roof. The Kiva has been a part of the culture and ceremonial life of the people of the Southwest since before the golden ages of Mesa Verde, Casa Bonito, and Chaco Canyon.

Ruff The ruff covers the edge of the case mask at the neck of the kachina. The ruff may consist of fir or spruce boughs, fur, or in some cases, feathers.

Sash/Belt Many kachinas wear a belt, which is usually red with black designs. The Crow Bride wears a belt which is white. The sash worn by most kachinas is woven of white cotton and has elaborate designs embroidered in wool on both ends of the sash.

Speaking Tube Many kachinas have a tube-shaped mouth that serves to amplify and disguise the voice of the kachina as they sing or chant.

Women's Robe Woven from white cotton with green and black wool embroidery on the top and bottom edges.

Yucca Whip Whips made of yucca leaves are used in initiation ceremonies.

The Crow Bride is nearly identical to the Crow Mother, but she is dressed entirely in white and carries a bowl of corn.

Kachinas for infants

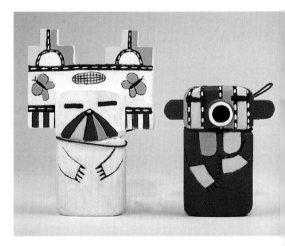

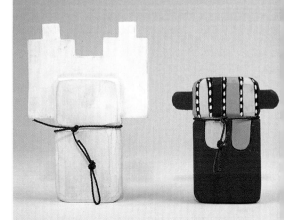

Gallery

Corn Dancer - Rugan

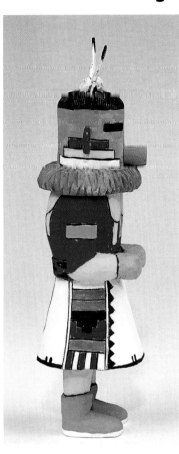
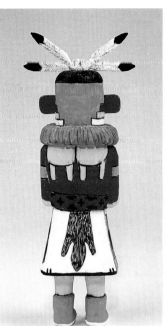

Poli Sio Hemis - Butterfly

Wolf - Kweo

Eagle - Kwahu

Broad Face

 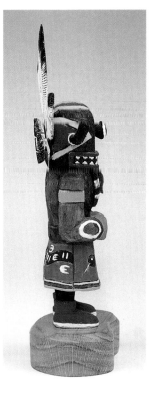  

Morning Kachina as Giver by Joe Moore

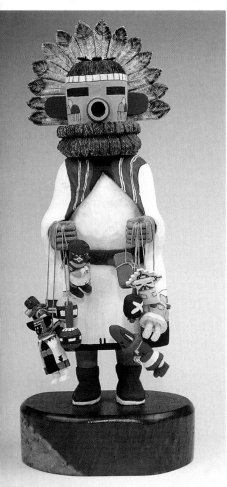   

Hochani

Salako Taka

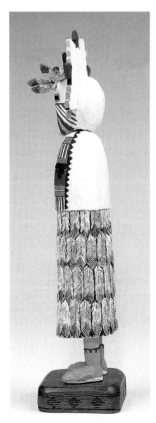   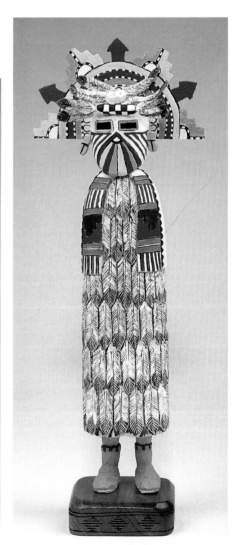